The Brand Identity exists to empower and support the graphic design industry.

the-brandidentity.com

Special thanks to Bienal, Collins, DesignStudio, DIA, Franklyn, Hype Type Studio, Passport, POST—, Public-Library, SocioDesign, Vertigo and Yuta Takahashi for their contributions.

Typeset in RM Pro by CoType Foundry.

Printed on Fedrigoni Sirio Ultra Black 370g/m2 and Fedrigoni Arena White Smooth 120g/m2.

Printed by Graphius in Ghent, Belgium.

All images © of their respective owners.

No part of this publication may be reproduced in any shape or form by any means, electronic or manual, including recording, photocopy or any informational storage and retrieval system, without prior permission from the copyright holder.

T 310.253.3300
M 323.395.4608

3542 Hayden Avenue
Culver City, CA 90232
info@it3am.com
www.it3am.com

To:
Hype Type Studio®
5356 Irvington Place
Los Angeles
CA 90042
USA

Date:
7 Oct 2014

Dear Sir,

Curabitur ultrices nisl vitae nunc vestibulum aliquet. Aliquam erat volutpat. Cras ac sem sit amet tellus dapibus pharetra in at urna. Curabitur non arcu mi. Etiam lacinia, mauris eget accumsan pellentesque, lorem tellus congue dolor, vitae vestibulum ipsum ipsum id lorem. Aliquam justo lacus, tempus vitae rutruma, eget metus.

Aliquam ultricies, libero nec rhoncus suscipit, dui nulla dapibus odio, eu iaculis nisi ligula nec purus. Curabitur ac mi neque, nec dignissim dolor. Nam sagittis velit et nisi suscipit non fermentum turpis porta. In hac habitasse platea dictumst. Aliquam ante massa, semper in placerat et, volutpat sit amet libero. Nulla facilisi. In dapibus tortor et felis interdum euismod.

Pellentesque quis leo eget arcu blandit molestie ac vel felis. Nunc condimentum, enim non hendrerit volutpat, quam dolor eleifend magna, id pretium est dolor nec elit. Curabitur mollis ante in diam lobortis ut sollicitudin purus posuere. Suspendisse pellentesque hendrerit ipsum, viverra volutpat neque porttitor sed. Mauris eget nulla mauris, nec tempor nulla. Maecenas eu sapien eget libero commodo pharetra.

Yours Sincerely,

Chris Eyerman

Chris Eyerman
Creative Director

Chris Eyerman
Creative Director

3542 Hayden Avenue,
Culver City, CA 90232

T 310.253.3300
M 323.395.4608

chris.eyerman@its3am.com
www.its3am.com

Chris Eyerman
Creative Director

3542 Hayden Avenue
Culver City, CA 90232

3AM

chris.eyerman@its3am.com
www.its3am.com

T 310.253.3300
M 323.395.4608

3542 Hayden Avenue
Culver City, CA 90232
info@its3am.com
www.its3am.com

T 310.253.3300
M 323.395.4608

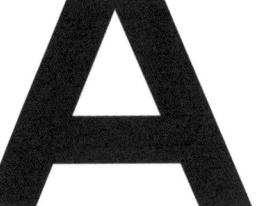

Date:
7 Oct 2014

To:
Hype Type Studio®
5356 Irvington Place
Los Angeles
CA 90042
USA

Dear Sir,

Curabitur ultrices nisl vitae nunc vestibulum aliquet. Aliquam erat volutpat. Cras ac sem sit amet tellus dapibus pharetra in at urna. Curabitur non arcu mi. Etiam lacinia, mauris eget accumsan pellentesque, lorem tellus congue dolor, vitae vestibulum ipsum ipsum id lorem. Aliquam justo lacus, tempus vitae rutruma, eget metus.

Aliquam ultricies, libero nec rhoncus suscipit, dui nulla dapibus odio, eu iaculis nisi ligula nec purus. Curabitur ac mi neque, nec dignissim dolor. Nam sagittis velit et nisi suscipit non fermentum turpis porta. In hac habitasse platea dictumst. Aliquam ante massa, semper in placerat et, volutpat sit amet libero. Nulla facilisi. In dapibus tortor et felis interdum euismod.

Aliquam ante massa, semper in placerat et, volutpat sit amet libero. Nulla facilisi. In dapibus tortor et felis interdum euismod.

Yours Sincerely,

Chris Eyerman

Chris Eyerman
Creative Director

Chris Eyerman
Creative Director

3542 Hayden Avenue,
Culver City, CA 90232

chris.eyerman@its3am.com
www.its3am.com

T 310.253.3300
M 323.395.4608

3AM
by Hype Type Studio

The Process

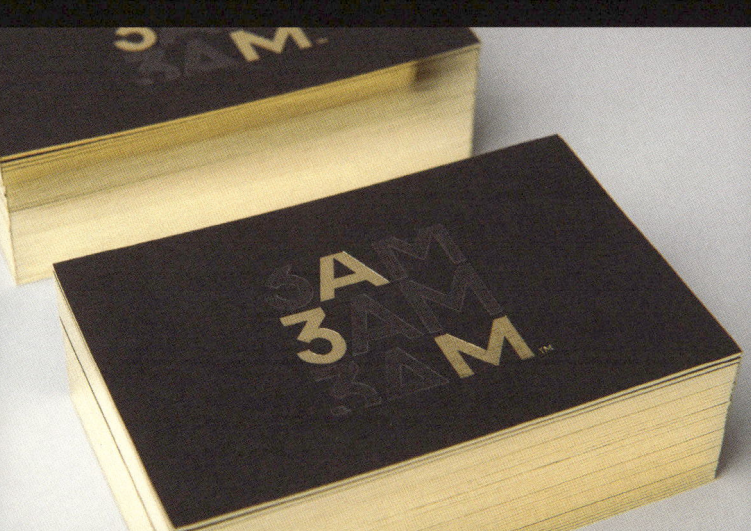

3AM
by Hype Type Studio

The Solution

3AM is a partnership between Ridley Scott's commercial production company RSA Films and movie ad agency Wild Card.

The firm develops new forms of content for global audiences and serves as a consultancy that collaborates with filmmakers, studios and brands in the early stages of a movies production to create integrated content and marketing extensions.

WARIMBA

WARIMBA

WARIMBA

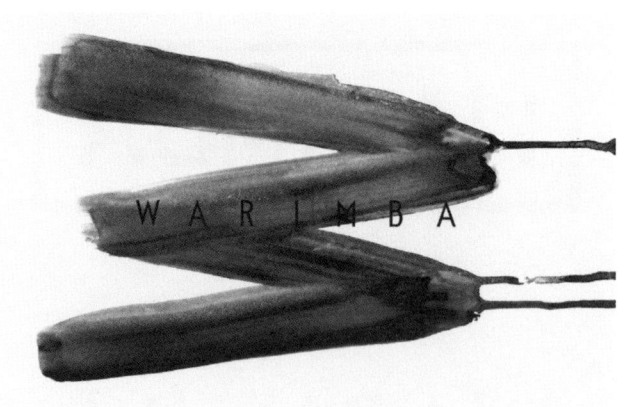

WARIMBA

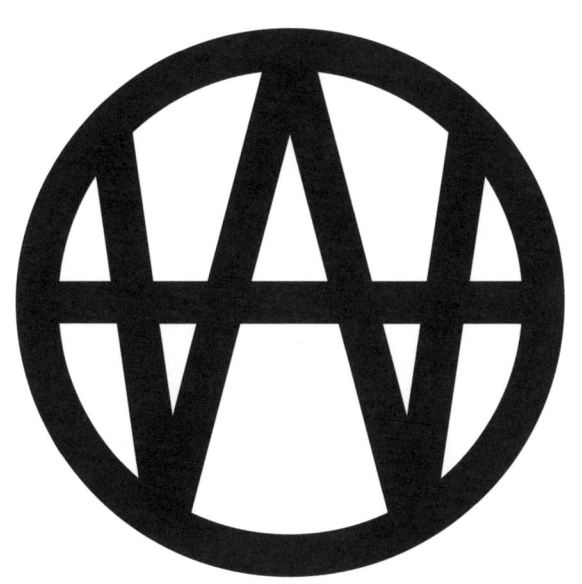

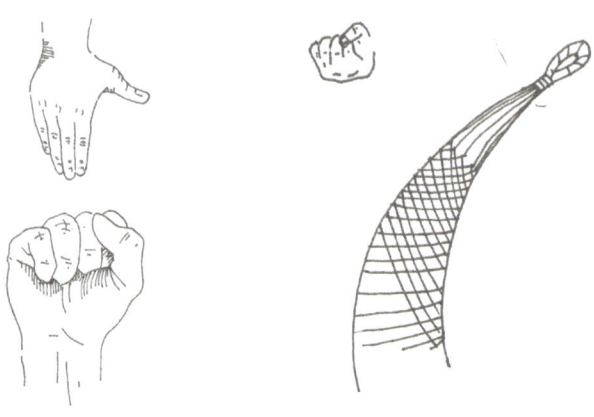

Warimba
by Bienal

The Process

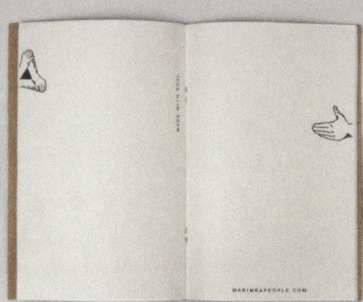

Warimba
by Bienal

The Solution

Warimba is an international hammock brand, based in Miami. The design of the hammocks is influenced by the Maya and Wayuu cultures of Latin America known for their wealth.

Warimba comes from the Venezuelan slang 'Guarimba', which means 'safe place' and in recent decades is a term used in protest against the dictatorial government.

The logo is inspired by the Wayuu knitting and the accompanying series of illustrations convey the values and brand personality.

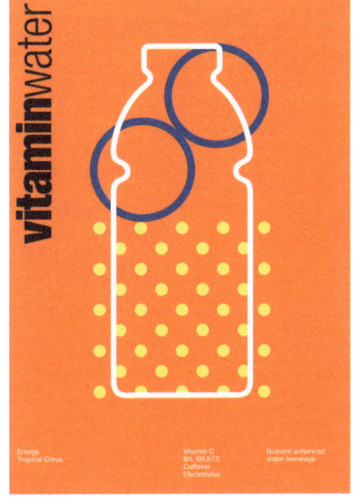

vitaminwater
by Collins

The Process

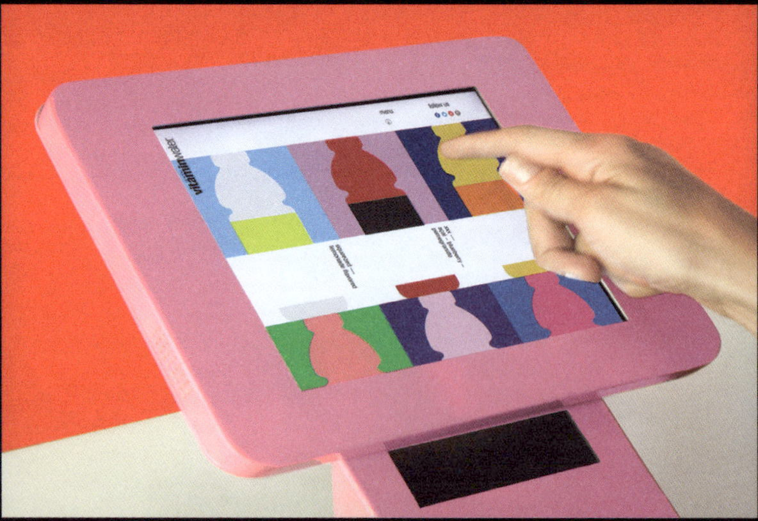

vitaminwater by Collins

The Solution

Established in 2000, vitaminwater is an iconic range of flavoured beverages which are available globally.

Collins reinvigorated the brand with life enhancing variety, bold simplicity and vibrant colour.

The Collins team for this project included Ben Crick, Leo Porto, Esther Li, Clay Kippen, Nicky Tesla, Leland Maschmeyer and Brian Collins.

Socio Design — Tenant Calculations — Executed 26th August — 2014

Compiled by
Stevenson Systems, Inc.
27822 El Lazo Road
Laguna Niguel, CA 92677

P: 1.949.297.4200
F: 1.949.297.4242
info@stevensonsystems.com
www.stevensonsystems.com

Skyler L.
Stevenson
— CEO

27822 El Lazo Rd
Laguna Niguel
CA 92677

DL: (949) 297-4207
FX: (949) 297-4242

skyler@
stevensonsystems
.com

stevensonsystems
.com

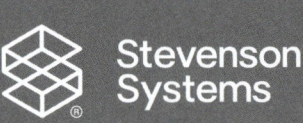

Stevenson Systems

27822 El Lazo Road
Laguna Niguel
CA 92677

DL: (949) 297-4200
FX: (949) 297-4242

info@
stevensonsystems
.com

www.
stevensonsystems
.com

Socio Design
61 Charterhouse Street
Farringdon
London
EC1M 6HA
UK.

Ref: Studio No.1, EC1M 6HA

Dear Sir,

Curabitur ultrices nisl vitae nunc vestibulum aliquet. Aliquam erat volutpat. Cras ac sem sit amet tellus dapibus pharetra in at urna. Curabitur non arcu mi. Etiam lacinia, mauris eget accumsan pellentesque, lorem tellus congue dolor, vitae vestibulum ipsum id lorem. Aliquam justo lacus, tempus vitae rutrum a, aliquam eget metus.

Aliquam ultricies, libero nec rhoncus suscipit, dui nulla dapibus odib, eu iaculis nisi ligula nec purus. Curabitur ac mi neque, nec dignissim dolor. Nam sagittis velit et nisi suscipit non fermentum turpis porta. In hac habitasse platea dictumst. Aliquam ante massa, semper in placerat et, volutpat sit amet libero. Nulla facilisi. In dapibus tortor et felis interdum euismod.

Pellentesque quis leo eget arcu blandit molestie ac vel felis. Nunc condimentum, enim non hendrerit volutpat, quam dolor eleifend magna, id pretium est dolor nec elit. Curabitur mollis ante in diam lobortis ut sollicitudin purus posuere. Suspendisse pellentesque hendrerit ipsum, viverra volutpat neque porttitor sed. Mauris eget nulla mauris, nec tempor nulla. Maecenas eu sapien eget libero commodo pharetra.

Quisque posuere egestas sapien, et porttitor tellus accumsan vel. Sed vel mauris nec lorem blandit pharetra. Suspendisse potenti. Nulla facilisi. Sed rutrum dolor

Yours Sincerely,

Skyler L. Stevenson
— CEO

Socio Developments
Tenant Calculations
Compiled
26th August
— 2014

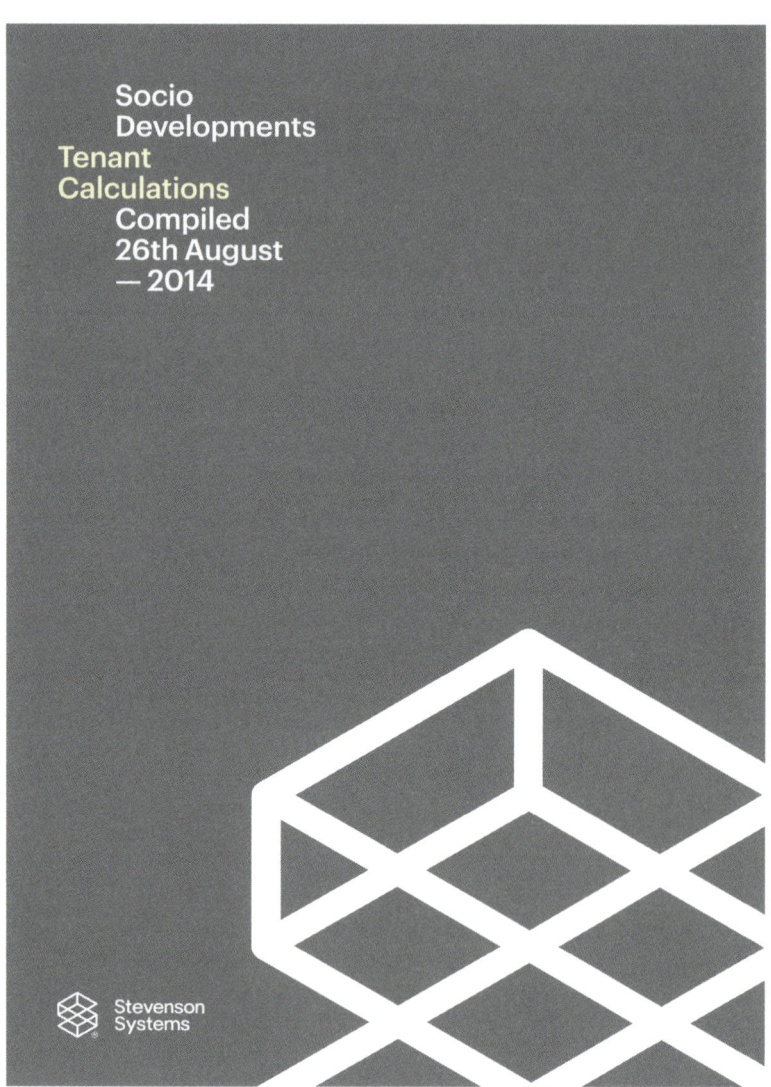

Stevenson Systems

CERTIFIED
SPACE ACCOUNTING

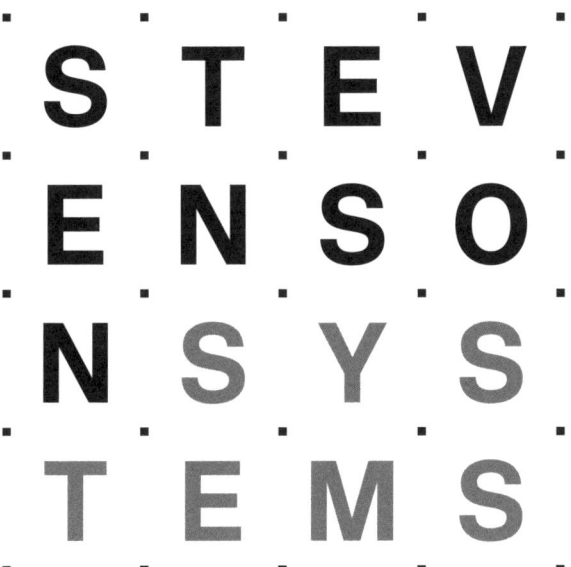

 Stevenson Systems

 Stevenson Systems

 Stevenson Systems

 Stevenson Systems

Stevenson Systems
by SocioDesign

The Process

Profile   Stories   Lifecycle   Services   Products   News   Contact   Request a Calculation

Senior Staff

Founder and President —
Peter L. Stevenson

Director of Performance
Development —
Mathew Romano

Project Manager —
Brandon Wightman

Project Manager —
Anthony Tumminia

Stevenson Systems by SocioDesign

The Solution

Stevenson Systems are a Space Accountancy firm based in Los Angeles. Stevenson Systems approached SocioDesign to create a new brand identity that would solidify their reputation as global leaders in the Space Accounting field and future proof the business from competing firms.

Socio designed a new marque that references the three dimensional properties of architectural spaces through a stacked isometric 'S'. This is complemented by a custom logotype with matching line weights, drawn to highlight the precision of laser measurement.

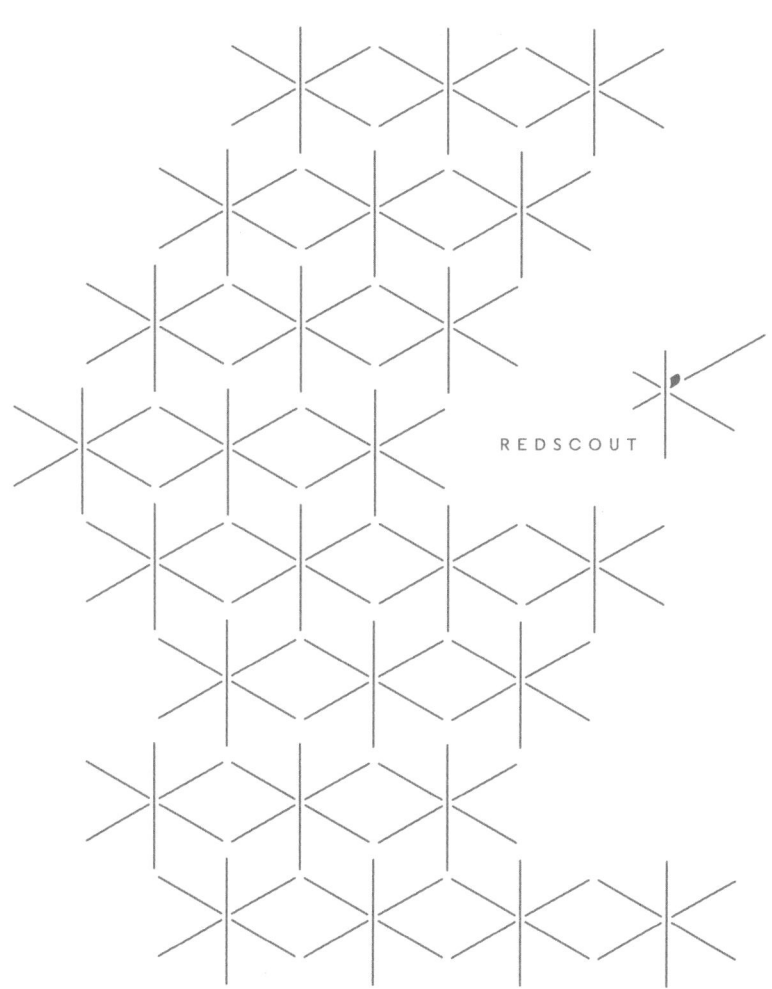

RED
SCOUT

INNOVATION
IS
THE
MOST
POWERFUL
FORM
OF
MARKETING

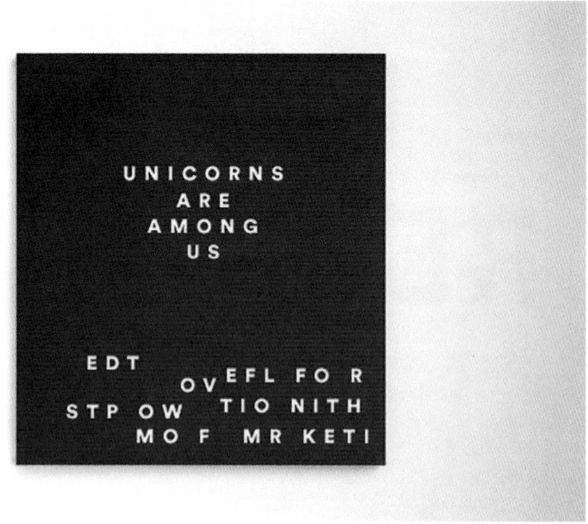

UNICORNS
ARE
AMONG
US

EDT   OV EFL FO R
STP OW TIO NITH
    MO F MR KETI

```
  E C O
TURDS
```

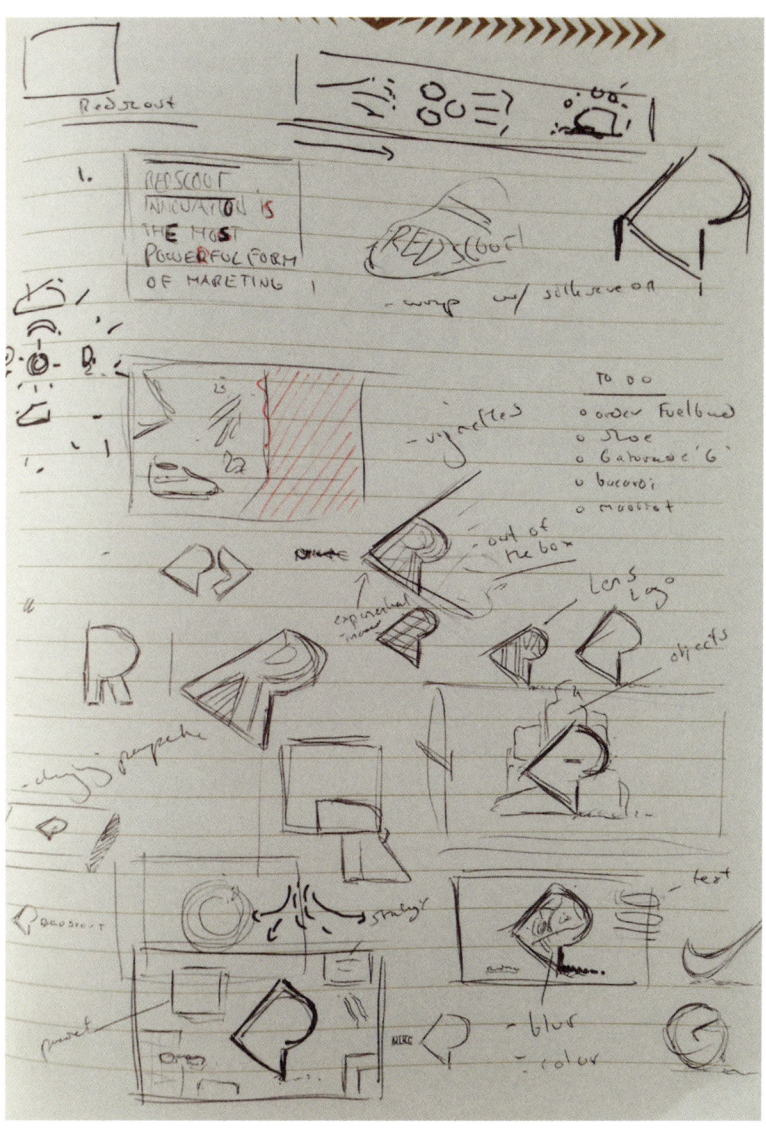

Redscout by Franklyn

The Process

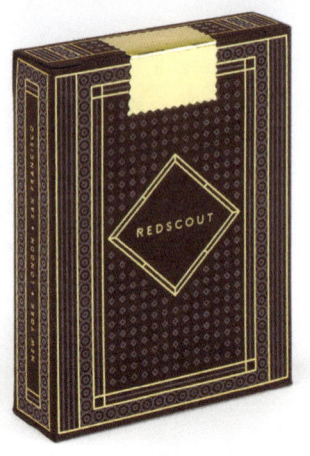

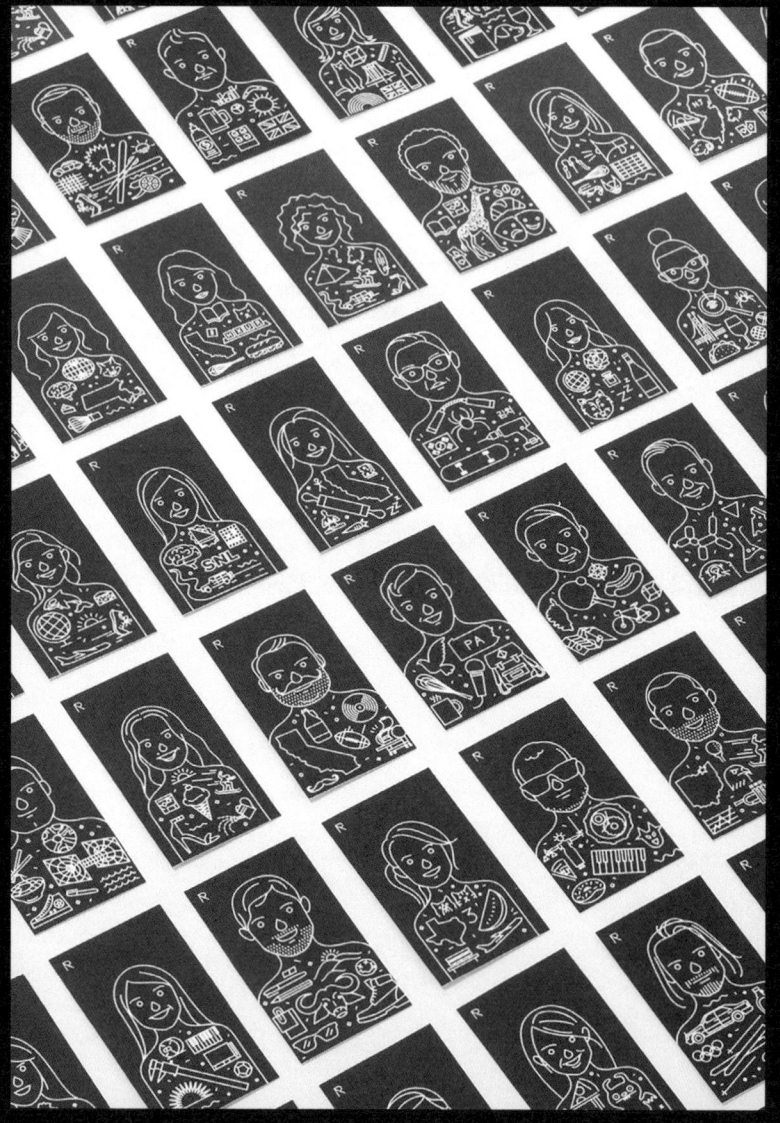

Redscout
by Franklyn

The Solution

An inherently mysterious agency serving as a behind-the-scenes brand shrink for companies in need of a fresh perspective, Redscout wanted to develop its own public image.

Inspired by their diverse team of loyal strategists and designers, Franklyn created a new identity system highlighting the diverse backgrounds and interests of their staff. Stylised illustrations of each employee were decorated with iconographic tattoos representing the who, what and where of these talented individuals.

r
e d

Holly Ross, Founder & Sales, Holly@redrep.tv, T. 310-253-3000, M. 323-610-8888, redrep.tv.

r
e d

Holly Ross, Founder & Sales, Holly@redrep.tv, T 310-253-3000, M 323-610-8888, redrep.tv.

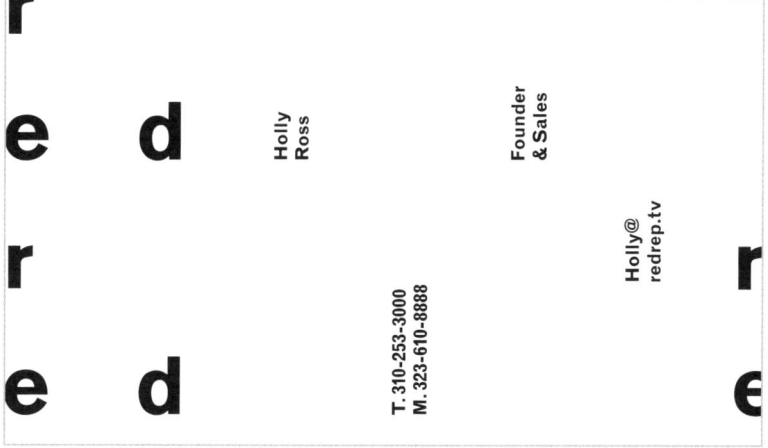

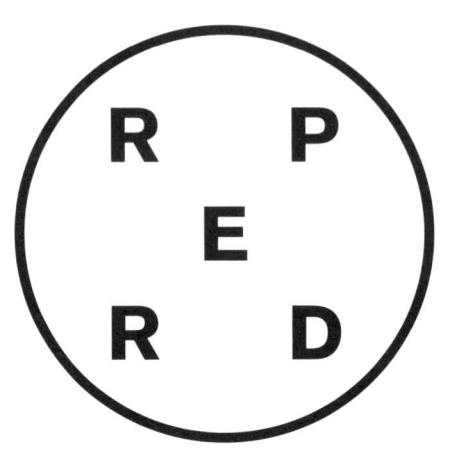

Red
Rep

Red

red

Red
by Public-Library

The Process

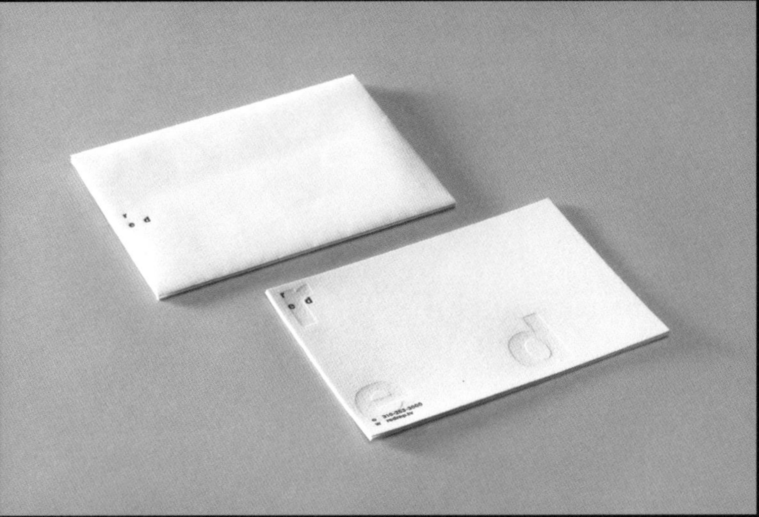

Red
by Public-Library

The Solution

Red represents a diverse group of directors and artists that make commercials, branded content, and experiential projects.

Public-Library created a structure-focused brand that allows Red to lead, as well as support, depending on the dynamic of the moment. Red is a company which exists invisibly to those outside the industry, but a company whose function and guidance create infinite opportunities. This concept was visualised through layering, alignments, and textural mixtures.

RAMBLING MUSE

THE ABSURDITY OF LIFE

RAMBLING MUSE

THE ABSURDITY OF LIFE

RAMBLING MUSE

RAMBLING MUSE

RAMBLING MUSE

RAMBLING MUSE

Rambling Muse
by SocioDesign

The Process

RAMBLING MUSE

GO
LINGER
GET

New York *facts:* Baby it's freezing!

Needless to say that I have never considered London a bastion of warmth or a tropical haven if you will. But that was before I started to get the New York facts transatlantically: baby it's freezing out there!

Having booked my tickets ages ago for this coming week, there was no doubt in my mind that the ice would thaw by that time so to speak. That the all knowing cold would briskly move it along in preparation for my arrival. That said, most unfortunately, this has not seemed to have happened. Sometimes hearsay is the worse. Sometimes however, it's just friends and family trying to warn someone who gets very cold very quickly of what lies ahead. Like doom and gloom!

Lorem ipsum dolor sit amet, consectetur adipisicing elit, do eiusmod tempor incididunt ut labore et

For instance, my mother literally told me point blank not to come. That it was simply unbearable. That said, she doesn't wear fur so I immediately dismissed the above directive. Of course, my subsequent thoughts were that New Yorkers should go back to the fur coats of the seventies and quit being so politically correct about dead animals. After all what can be so bad when you look like a little polar bear skidding through the arctic tundra? Well besides falling through the ice into the deadly waters... But no fur for me- I cannot bear the thought of getting egged like Anna Wintour.

Freely wondering New York, is the best way to find gems.

A must visit, Brookly Bridge.

Then, my good New York friend told me that no one goes out anymore. Restaurants are empty... just of course not the ones we tried to book for a Friday night out. Apparently, the city is deserted as people huddle inside to keep warm. To be honest, I definitively at first attributed all of this to my entourage's

RAMBLING MUSE

GO
LINGER
GET

Taxi service or Uber in London, Paris, Berlin and New York

TRAVEL TALES

Latest Ramblings

View All

Catch of the day: Fresh Tuna

GO/EAT

When first heading to the coast I came across an old friend...

Great Britain and the Union: yay or ney?!

LINGER/TRAVEL TALES

Opinion divided. Where do you stand on the EU opinion polls...

Taxi service or Uber in London, Paris Berlin NYE

LINGER/TRAVEL TALES

Needless to say I have never considered New York...

Treat yourself! My favourite cocktail to have in the Savoy

LINGER/TRAVEL TALES

Ok, for once I had to just pop in and indulge a little...

Travelling through Japan the fastest train in the world: the speedy bullet train

LINGER/TRAVEL TALES

Needless to say that I have never considered... London a

Great park expanses in New York and beyond...

LINGER/TRAVEL TALES

Catching the right amount of me time can be difficult...

RAMBLING MUSE

Mr James Rutter
Studio BM
30 Great Guildford St.
London, SE1 0HS.

Dear James,

I am just writing to you to inform you of the great feedback that I have had for your vase that was listed last week. I have inundated with purchase requests and will happily pass this information on should you wish to continue down the e-commerce route.

As always its been a pleasure featuring your work on Rambling Muse and would happily do this again should you wish to in the near future.

Best of luck with the this years new show!

Yours Sincerely,

Polly Dugdale
Rambling Muse

Rambling Muse
by SocioDesign

The Solution

Rambling Muse is a lifestyle blog providing views of London life, witty commentaries on news and politics, recipes and product features, from writer Clarisse Lehmann.

Having lived in New York, Geneva, Tokyo, Madrid and now London, Clarisse's perspective as an 'outsider in the city' provided inspiration for the brand identity – the logo depicts the Little Owl, a non-native species introduced to the UK in the nineteenth century. The owl also represents a keen eye for observation and is culturally seen as wise and informed.

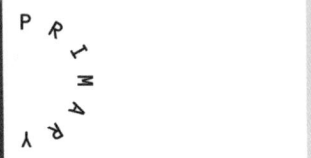
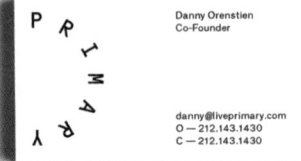

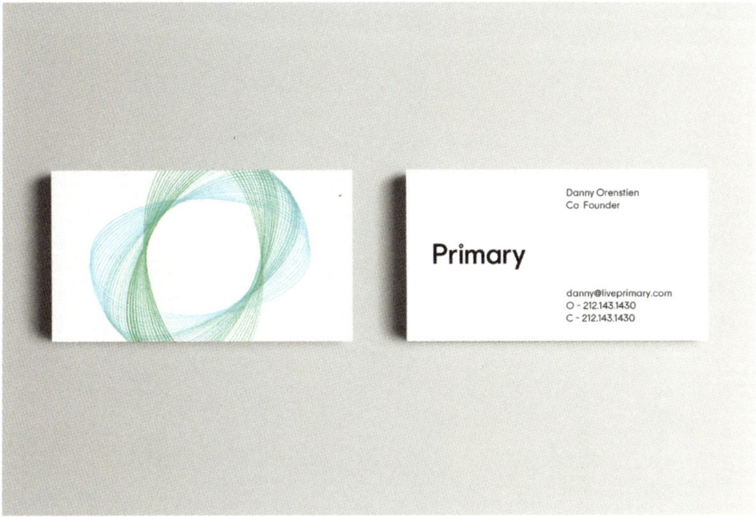

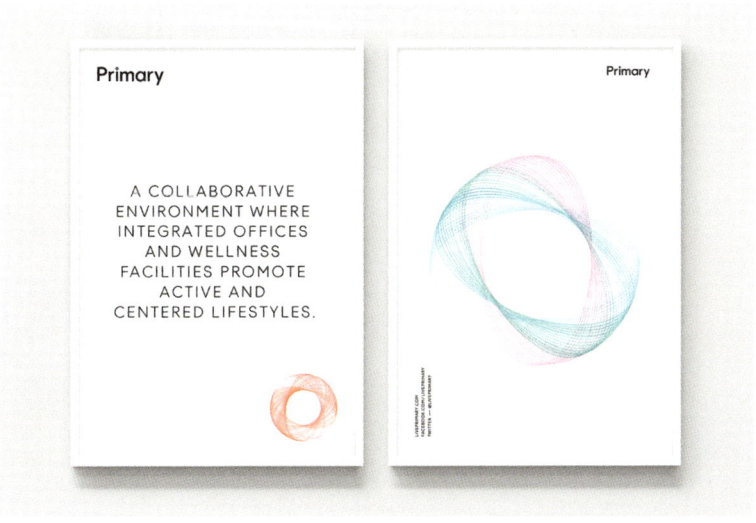

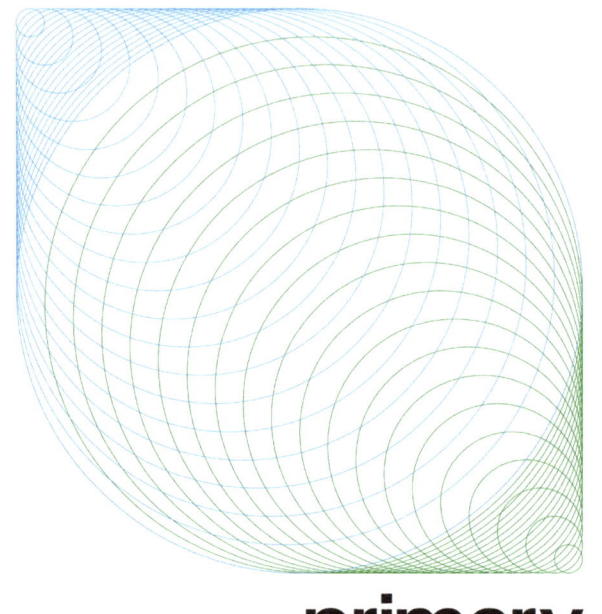

primary

Primary
by DIA

The Process

Primary
by DIA

The Solution

Primary is a new co-working concept that blends health and wellness into the workplace. DIA were tasked with creating a sophisticated but approachable identity that resonates with Primary's health conscious and savvy entrepreneur audience.

The identity is based on specific colour psychology. DIA developed a generative based platform that creates unique logos depending on desired moods or time of day.

LIFT

LIFT

LIFT

Lift

Lift

Lift

 Lift

```
L I
F T
```

LIFT LIFT

[L I F T]

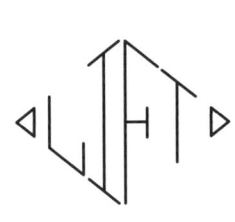

Lift by EnCore
by Hype Type Studio

The Process

LIFT

Lift by EnCore
by Hype Type Studio

The Solution

Hype Type Studio were commissioned to create the brand and visual identity for Lift by EnCore. Lift is the commercial aircraft seating division of the EnCore group based in California.

EnCore serves the commercial aerospace and defence sectors with a broad range of products including seats, interiors and composite aircraft structures. The Lift seats are setting industry bench marks for quality and comfort and in the process have redefined the narrative of economy class seating.

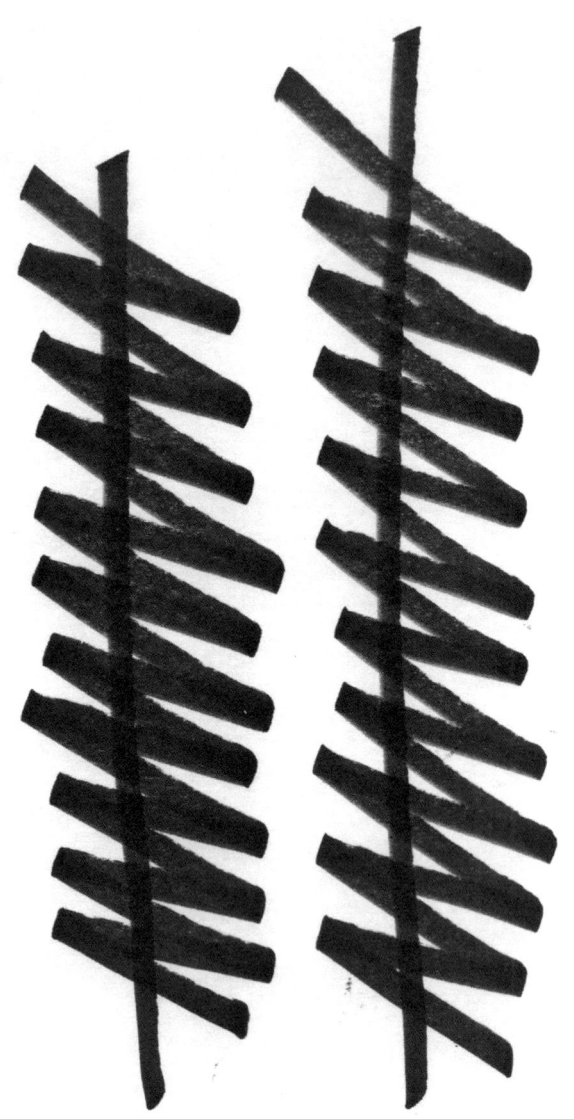

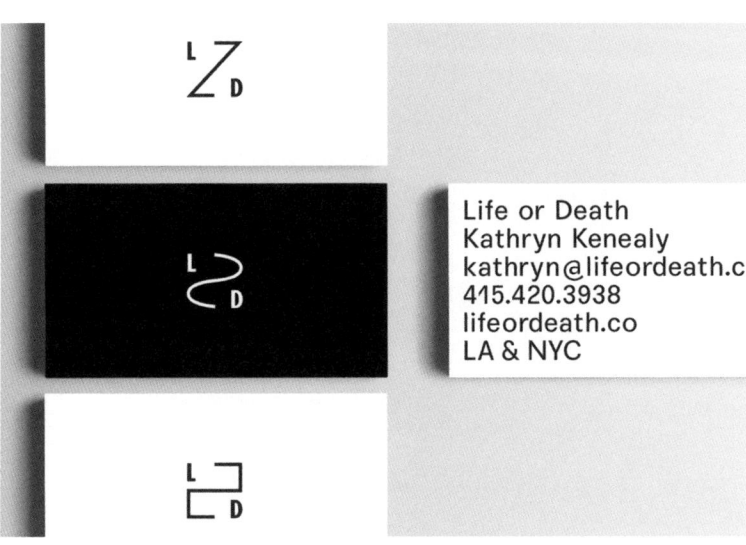

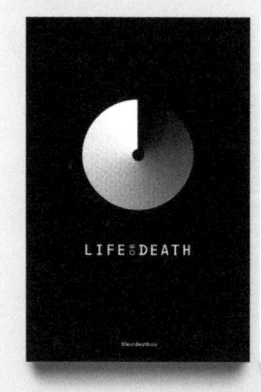

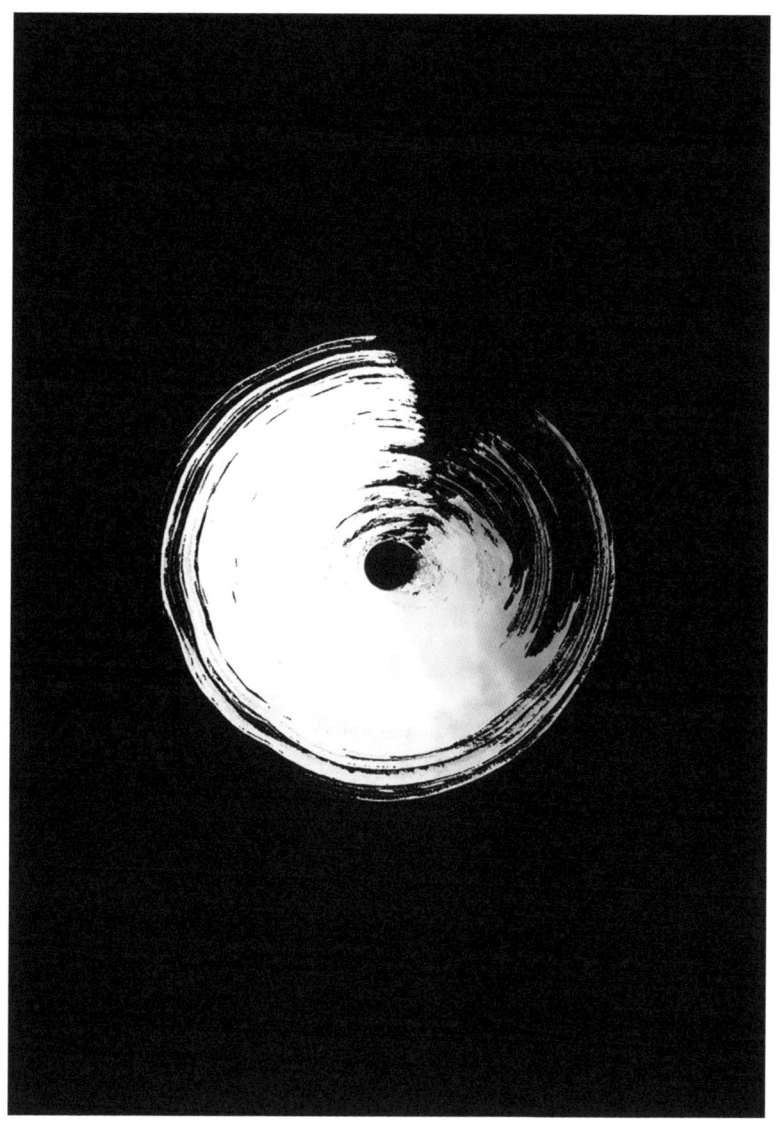

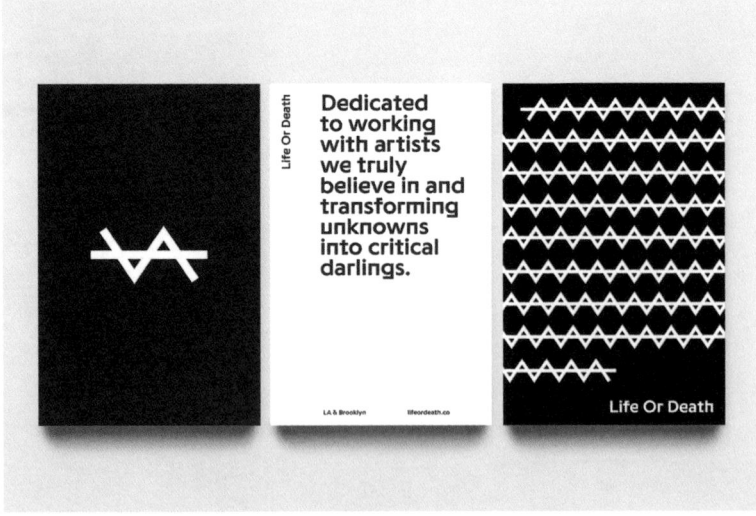

Life or Death by DIA

The Process

MIKKY EKKO

E FREAKER

TRICKY

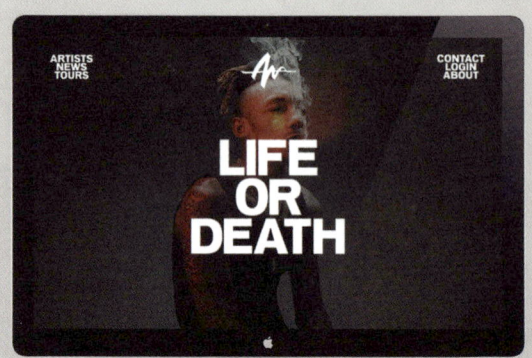

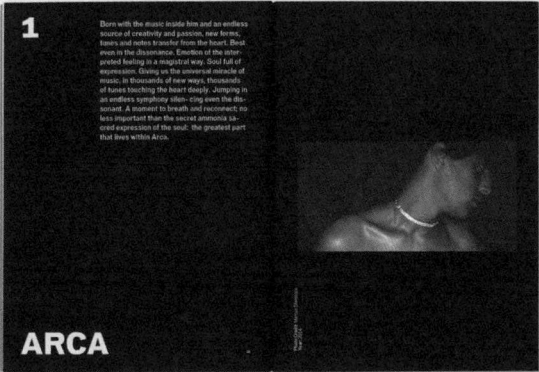

1

Born with the music inside him and an endless source of creativity and passion, new forms, tunes and notes transfer from the heart. Beat even in the dissonance. Emotion of the interpreted feeling in a magistral way. Soul full of expression. Giving us the universal miracle of music. In thousands of new ways, thousands of tunes touching the heart deeply. Jumping in an endless symphony silencing even the dissonant. A moment to breath and reconnect; no less important than the secret ammonia sacred expression of the soul: the greatest part that lives within Arca.

ARCA

Life or Death by DIA

The Solution

Life or Death is a full-service public relations and management firm. With foundations in representing musicians, they've since expanded into fashion, art and writing. DIA's goal was to create an artistic and fashionable identity while honouring their hip hop roots.

The logo is a combination of both a heart rate monitor and a sound wave. Additionally, the logo was designed to be like a graffiti tag, so it can be rendered in infinite ways with a marker or brush.

KO/Photographic

KO/Videography

KO/Retouching

KO/Special Effects

KO/Productions

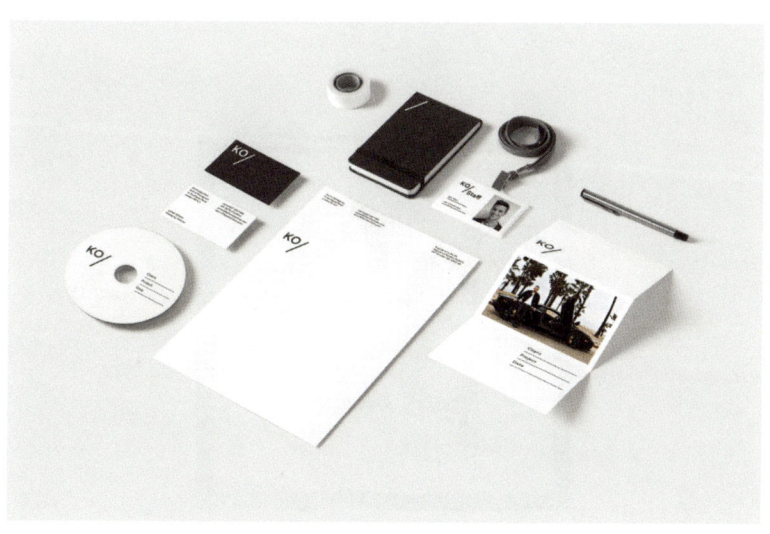

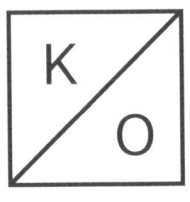 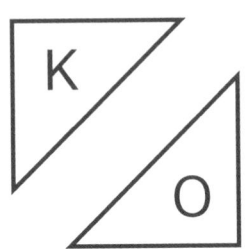

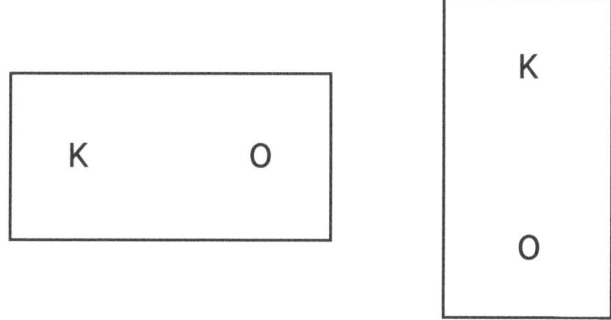

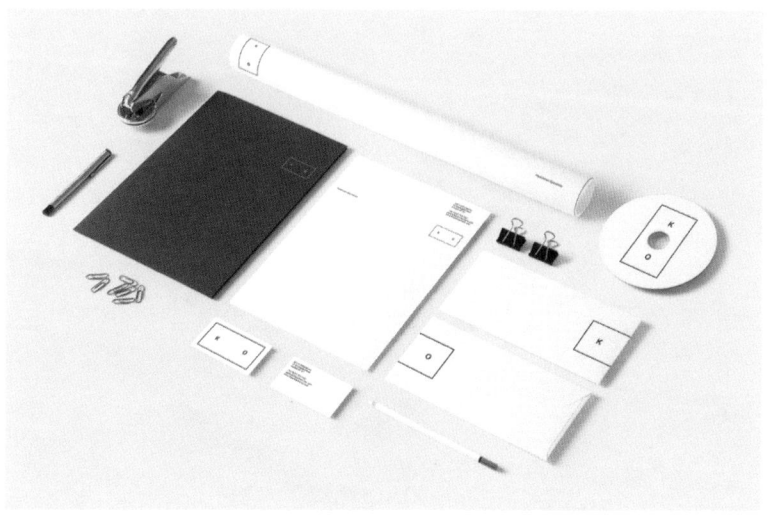

KO

KOKIOKIK
OKOIIKOKII

Katy **O**ffley
—Production Specialists

K   O
—Production Specialists

K   O
**   P**
S

KO Productions by POST—

The Process

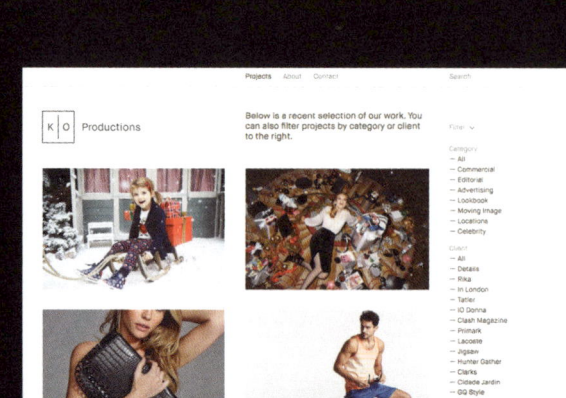

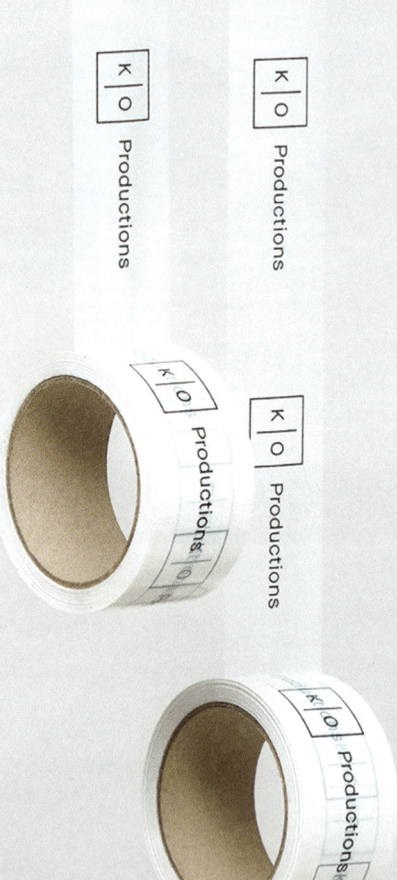

KO Productions by POST—

The Solution

KO are production specialists covering all aspects of photography and video, delivering professional content for leading brands. POST— were asked to re-design their identity and website alongside a comprehensive stationery suite and marketing materials.

The identity is a framework that can be adapted to specific services, as well as one that can evolve in unison with the company's expansion. Working predominantly in the fashion sector meant that a high-end aesthetic was required. This was reflected using premium textured materials with a mix of tactile print processes.

NUNOME, NARA
34°42'04.4"N - 135°58'38.6"E

NUNOME, NARA
34°42'04.4"N - 135°58'38.6"E

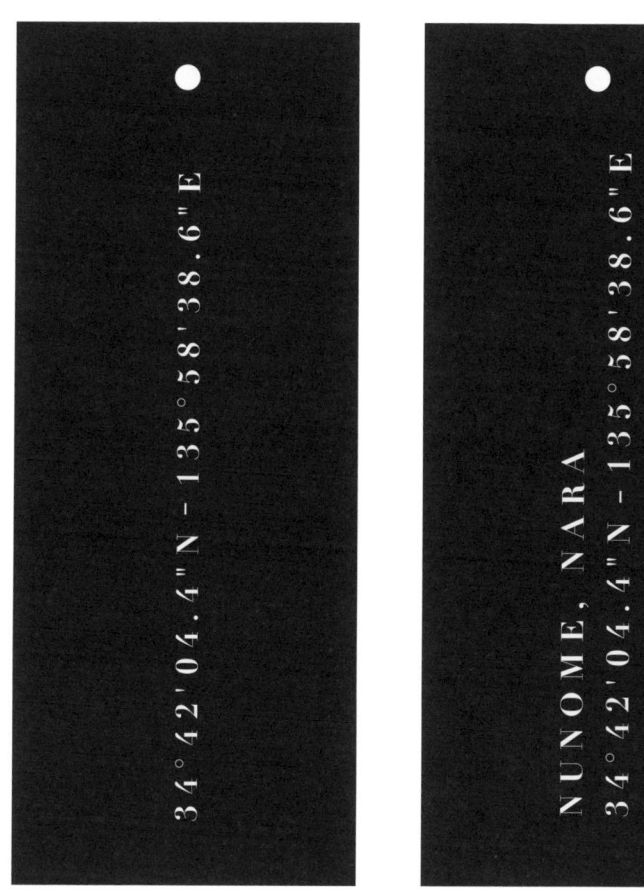

GUELL

GUELL

GUELL

GUELL

GUELL

GUELL	GUELL
Guell	Guell
guell	guell
GUELL	GUELL
Guell	Guell
guell	guell

Guell
by Yuta Takahashi

The Process

GUELL

Guell
by Yuta Takahashi

The Solution

Guell is a road-wear brand based in Japan.
With the rise in people involved in road biking,
there has recently been a demand for increased
diversity in road-wear.

Inspiration for the logotype was taken from
gears, speed, muscle movement, breathing,
and the light and shadows from the sun.

77

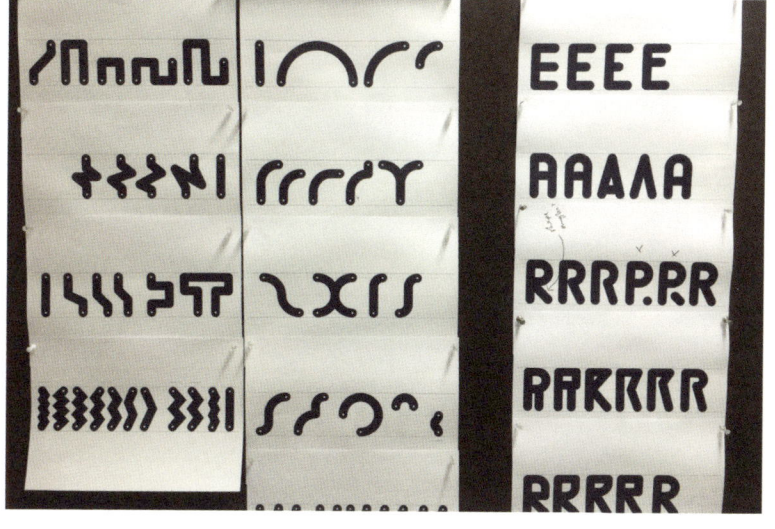

Future Finance
by DesignStudio

The Process

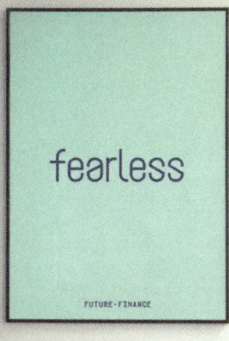
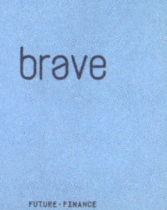

Hi, Millie

Your starter pack

FUTURE · FINANCE

Future Finance
by DesignStudio

The Solution

DesignStudio worked with Future Finance, the UK's biggest private student lender, to create a new identity for their brand. Future Finance help people fund their futures in smart, flexible ways, and have levelled the playing field so that everyone can rise up to their potential.

Using a joined-up language of ever moving lines, chevrons, curves and humps, their new identity focuses on the individual paths people take to achieve their goals. As no one student is the same, the identity is constantly moving, shifting and flexing – connecting people to their futures.

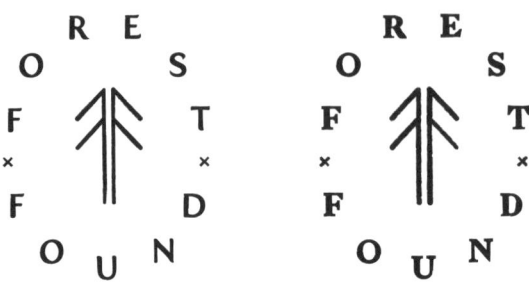

× FOREST FOUND ×

EST.2015

FOREST
FOUND

× FOREST FOUND ×

FOREST FOUND

Forest Found by Passport

The Process

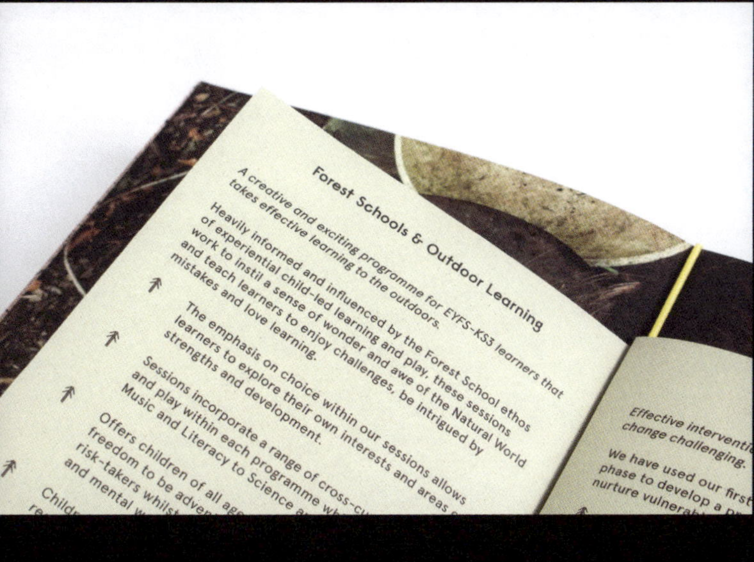

Forest Found
by Passport

The Solution

Forest Found works to get people of all ages and backgrounds outside. Having grown up climbing hills and adventuring in woodlands they want to pass on their enthusiasm for the powerful and tangible benefits of nature.

They approached Passport in search of a flexible and dynamic brand identity that could adapt to a multitude of different applications. They started with a humble tree that is built out of Forest Found's initials by way of back-to-back letter F's, which is complemented by customised typography that alludes to the growing branches and roots of the forest.

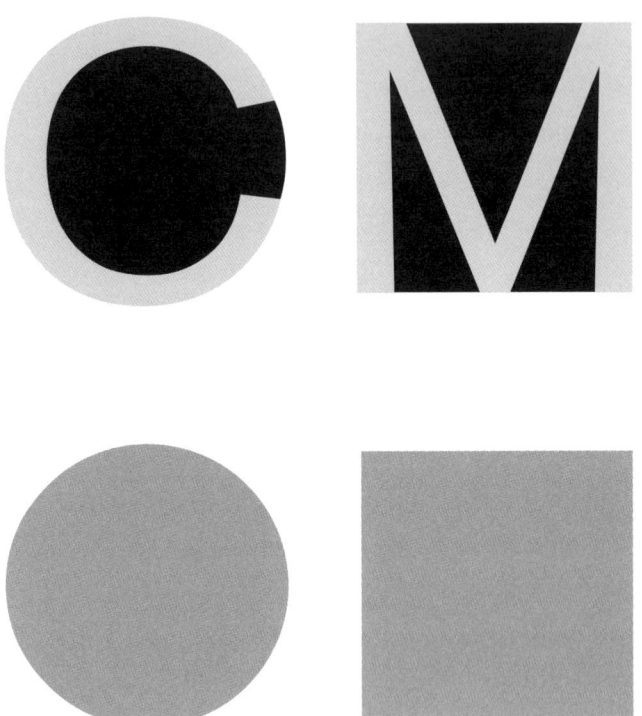

CreativeMoreland

CM

CreativeMoreland

CM

Creative Moreland by Vertigo

The Process

Creative Moreland is a community resource for local creative businesses and artists in the Moreland area of inner north Melbourne, Australia.

If you have a business, event, exhibition, workshop or class you would like to promote, email hello@creativemoreland.com.au or visit creativemoreland.com.au.

creativemoreland.com.au

● ■ Creative Moreland

Community Guide

●■ Creative Moreland

Creative Moreland is a community resource for creative businesses and artists in the Moreland area of inner north Melbourne, Australia.

Wilson Avenue

Launched in 2015, the new public space in Wilson Avenue, Brunswick, features landscaping, seating, urban bouldering wall, and graffiti and street art created by local Melbourne artists.

Public space

Wilson Avenue encourages gatherings and facilitates inspiration for many local artists, who come together to collaborate on projects, discuss ideas, and enjoy the fresh air and open space the area has to offer.

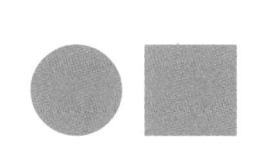

Creative Moreland

Tamara Russell
Curator

+61 423 042 867
hello@creativemoreland.com.au
creativemoreland.com.au

Creative Moreland by Vertigo

The Solution

Creative Moreland is a community resource for creative businesses and artists in the Moreland area of Melbourne to discover, collaborate with and promote each other.

The new identity helps build the brand's presence in the community through a simple and memorable visual narrative, designed to appeal to established businesses, connect with new ones, and endure into the future as Moreland continues to grow in population and creative success.

CAPSULE

34

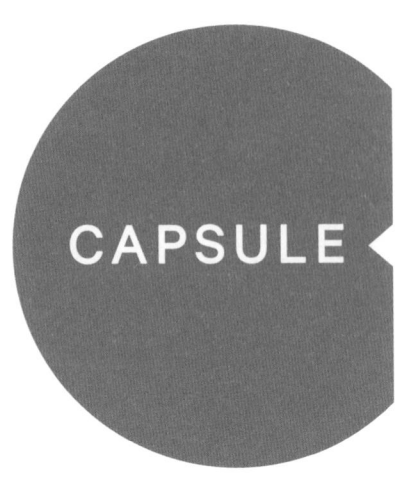

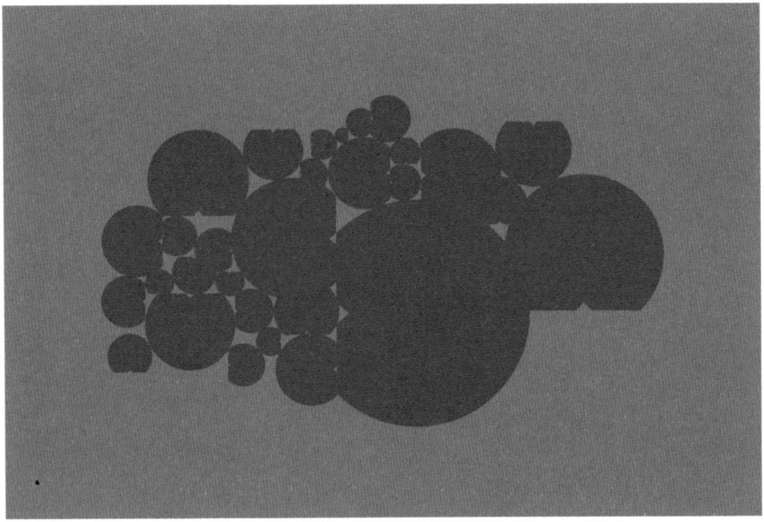

Capsule by Franklyn

The Process

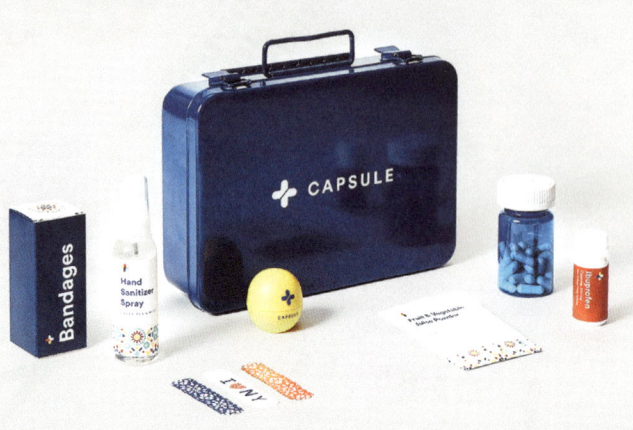

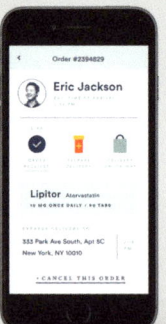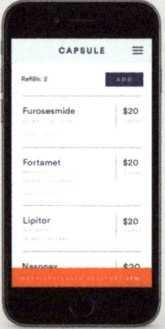

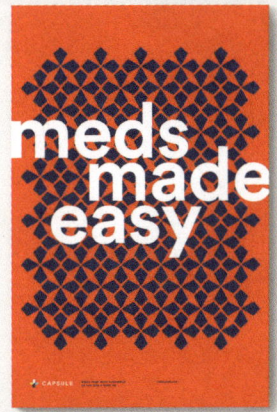

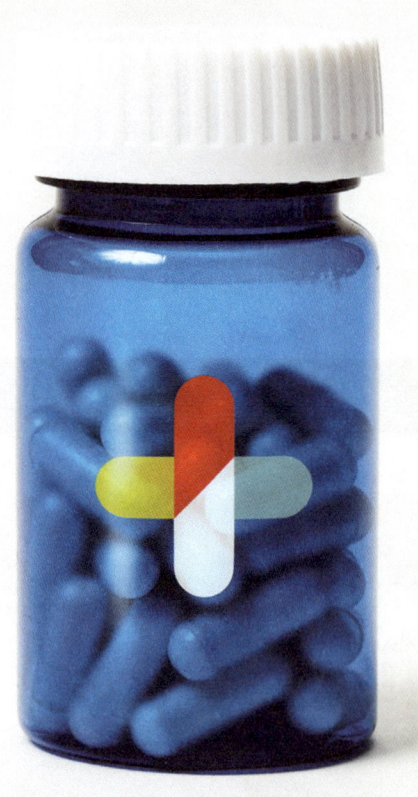

Capsule
by Franklyn

The Solution

A new kind of pharmacy, Capsule's prescription delivery service renders the highly inconvenient process of waiting in line at the pharmacy obsolete.

Franklyn developed a bold visual identity that successfully straddles the line between playful and professional. Extending the brand to all that a modern pharmacy needs to make its mark, they designed delivery bags, pill bottles, bandages, a website, digital app, billboards, subway takeovers and much, much more.

Happy making, happy hunting

Artfinder

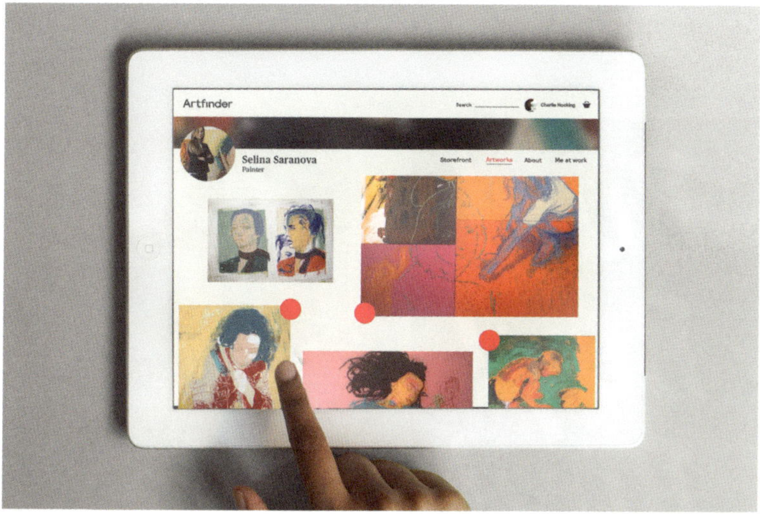

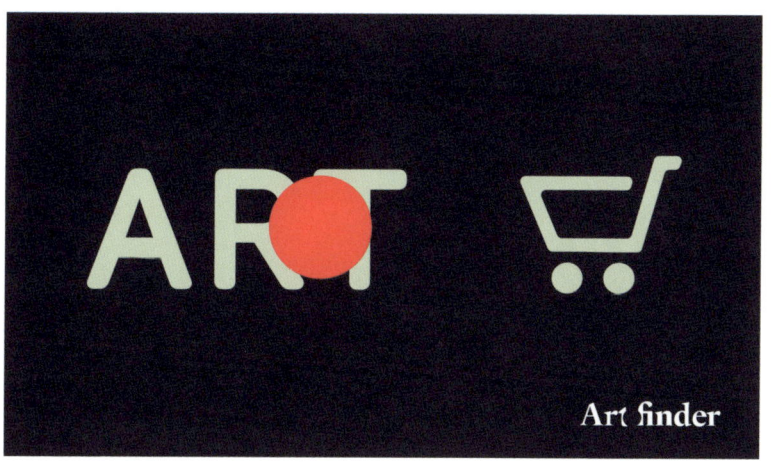

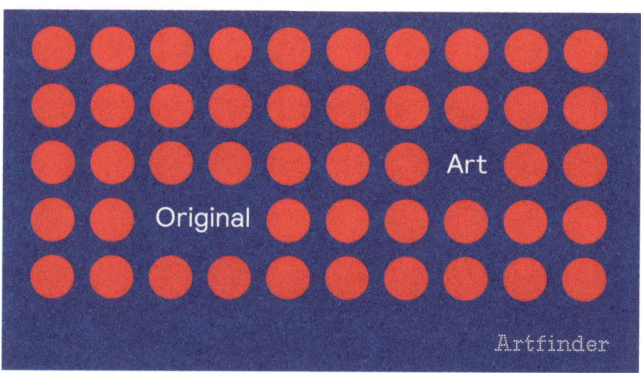

Original Art

Artfinder

We believe passionately that owning art will change your life and transf[orm] your space. Also, when you buy fr[om] Artfinder, you directly support arti[sts] around the world.

Artfinder

Making art work in your living room

Artfinder

Making artwork in your living room

Artfinder

Artfinder

Art finder

Artfinder
by DesignStudio

The Process

Artfinder

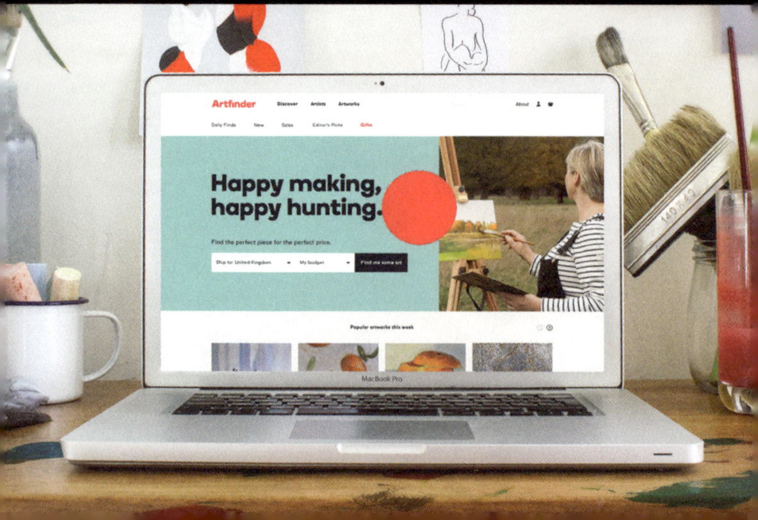

Artfinder
by DesignStudio

The Solution

DesignStudio worked with Artfinder, the art marketplace, to create a brand to amplify its ambitions.

Artfinder's dot reinterprets the language of the traditional art world. Without a fixed position, it overlaps imagery, colour blocks and text, while constantly scaling, cropping and flexing — the dot can be expressive to the point of being intrusive.

Warimba　　　　　　　　　　p210
by Bienal

3AM　　　　　　　　　　　p224
by Hype Type Studio

The Projects

Rambling Muse p142
by SocioDesign

Red p154
by Public-Library

Redscout p166
by Franklyn

Stevenson Systems p182
by SocioDesign

vitaminwater p198
by Collins

Guell   p80
by Yuta Takahashi

KO Productions   p90
by POST—

Life or Death   p104
by DIA

Lift by EnCore   p116
by Hype Type Studio

Primary   p130
by DIA

The Projects

Artfinder by DesignStudio	p10
Capsule by Franklyn	p26
Creative Moreland by Vertigo	p40
Forest Found by Passport	p52
Future Finance by DesignStudio	p68

Passport

Leeds, UK
wearepassport.com

POST—

London, UK
deliveredbypost.com

Public-Library

Los Angeles, USA
public-library.org

SocioDesign

London, UK
sociodesign.co.uk

Vertigo

Melbourne, AU
studiovertigo.com.au

Yuta Takahashi

Ehime, JP
yutatakahashi.jp

The Studios

Bienal

Yucatán, MX
bienal.mx

DIA

New York City, USA
dia.tv

Collins

New York City and
San Francisco, USA
wearecollins.com

Franklyn

New York City, USA
quitefranklyn.com

DesignStudio

London, UK and
San Francisco, USA
wearedesignstudio.com

Hype Type Studio

Los Angeles, USA
hypetypestudio.com

Behind every branding project there's dozens of ideas that never saw the light of day.

This book explores those ideas.

The Process

A book by The Brand Identity